MAKE YOUR PAYCHECK LAST

MAKE YOUR PAYCHECK
LAST

•SECOND EDITION•

By Harold Moe

THE CAREER PRESS
180 Fifth Ave.
PO Box 34
Hawthorne, NJ 07507

1-800-CAREER-1
201-427-0229 (Outside U.S.)
FAX: 201-427-2037

Make Your Paycheck Last, 2nd Ed.,
ISBN 1-56414-058-X, $8.95

To order by mail, please include price as noted above, $2.50 handling per order, plus $1.00 for each book ordered. Send to: Career Press, 180 Fifth Ave., PO Box 34, Hawthorne, NJ 07507. Or call Toll-Free 1-800-CAREER-1 to order using your VISA or Mastercard or for information on all books available from The Career Press.

IMPORTANT: While much careful thought and depth of research have been devoted to the writing of this book, all content is to be viewed as general information only and should not be construed as actual legal, accounting or financial advice of a personal nature.

The reader is urged to consult competent legal, accounting and tax advisors regarding all legal and personal financial decisions. This book is not meant to be utilized as a substitute for their advice.

"Men do not realize how great an income thrift is."

—*Cicero*

"Annual income 20 pounds, annual expenditure 19, 19, 6, result happiness. Annual income 20 pounds, annual expenditure 20, 0, 6, result misery."

—*Charles Dickens*

PRAISE FOR BOOK

People already using *Make Your Paycheck Last* say:

"I read about [your book] in The Wall Street Journal. The book fits my criteria for books that work."

—*WSJ reader, Oklahoma*

"Harold Moe's book, Make Your Paycheck Last, is a Godsend!"

—*Family, New Jersey*

"Retirement has not been (financially) easy, but after reading your book and putting your method to work, we are able to live without worry."

—*Retired, New Mexico*

"I am currently trying to start over again. Thanks to your book, it's working."

—*Bankrupt, Wisconsin*

"Reading your book together has made us a team."

—*Housewife, Tennessee*

"Thank you for your book and insight on financial success. My wife and I have been on your system one and a half months...we can see results happening and taking shape."

—*Michigan family*

"[We] purchased your book and were so impressed that we followed your instructions step by step. One of our five-year plans (a new house) is now within our reach. Our 'good luck' was due to your book and our dedication to manage our money instead of letting it slip through our fingers."

—*Teacher, Wisconsin*

"I have been using your book for almost two years now. I not only paid off (my) medical bills, but also managed to pay off two loans. It's the best and easiest method I know of on how to handle personal finance. I know I would never have made it this far without your book."

—*Reader, Nebraska*

"[Make Your Paycheck Last] very simply is the best book that both my wife and I have read on this subject to date. I think that if I had to pick a word to describe Harold's ideas, that word would have to be control."

—*Businessman, New Zealand*

"I would like to thank you for writing Make Your Paycheck Last. Thanks to your book and a lot of hard work, I opened my own business. As a single parent, I have been surviving, but I think it's about time to change that status, and I have visions that your book is part of the key."

—*Accountant, Virginia*

"Thank you for your wonderful book; it was a prayer from heaven. After reading the very first chapter, I can tell why it works."

—*Dentist, Israel*

"I have just finished reading your book [and] I am so excited. The reason is that [my husband] is retiring from the military this May and your [book] will help us enter into our civilian life with an organized plan for control and ideas."

—*Couple, Florida*

"I think your book helped save my marriage. With a $70,000-plus income, we were drowning under our bills. We still have a rough road ahead, but now we have control, and I know we're going to make it."

—*Writer, California*

"Your book is clear and simply written. More important, I didn't feel ashamed or stupid as I read it."

—*Military family, Germany*

"Thank you again, Your book is the only one on the market that helps the 'everyday' guy. Trust me, I know! I bought everything I could find."

—*Secretary, Washington, DC*

"I've been an office manager for 15 years. I handle all financial accounting for our firm, but for some reason, I couldn't apply my knowledge to our home finances. Thanks to your book, I now am as organized at home as I am at work."

—*Manager, Texas*

"At long last, we have the opportunity to do this book! It has changed our financial management in the most productive way! Thank you, Harold Moe."

—*Mother of two, Minnesota*

"Your books have changed our lives for the better. There are no more fights about money and the tension is gone."

—*Couple, Washington*

"Thanks for your understanding book,[and] another thanks for your workbook. For the first time in my financial life I understand needs versus wants."

—*Engineer, Canada*

"[After starting your system], this month I put $475 into my savings account. I still can hardly believe it. For the first time in my financial life, I feel like there is hope for me...I recommend [your book] to everyone now."

—*Flight attendant, California*

"To me, the most important tip from the book was to establish goals. Mr. Moe talks about goals throughout and could not have emphasized a better underlying principle of financial security."

—*Parent, Illinois*

"Thanks to you and your plan, I can see light at the end of the tunnel!"

—*Single parent, Minnesota*

"I love being in control! Believe me, if you earn a paycheck, you should have this book! Send another copy to a wayward friend!"

—*Airline employee, Illinois*

"I was doing fine until I took a 20-percent pay cut. Your book saved the day."

—*Worker, Florida*

"You must tell people! Your book does wonders. I have just returned from a vacation to Israel after using your strategy for only 18 months."

—*Nurse, Ohio*

"Have just finished one month with your book, and what an easy way to set up our finances."

—*Airline captain, Minnesota*

"The new 'luxuries' (weekend trips) are something we never would have been able to afford before we started using your plan. The children's educations and a new car are only part of the things we are saving for, instead of worrying about it. Thank you for your book."

—*Parent, Ohio*

"We've already done various things you've suggested in your book, but now I think it will all be drawn together into one solid plan."

—*Homemaker, Hawaii*

"I've read a lot of financial books. This one really works. My only regret is that I didn't buy this book first."
—*Executive, Wisconsin*

"This is the first time I have ever written anyone to tell them how excited I am about their product. Your book is the best thing that has happened to my paycheck."
—*Working single, Minnesota*

"I never dreamed anything would work for me. But, so far, so good."
—*Secretary, Texas*

More praise from the professionals who use and recommend *Make Your Paycheck Last*

"We are, on a very systematic basis, introducing the Make Your Paycheck Last system to all of our clients. It is without a doubt the best organized system we have ever seen."
—*Certified Financial Planner, Indiana*

"I am so excited with your approach. It overcomes the deep psychological blocks most of us have and really frees people to use their money unemotionally."
—*Credit union, Illinois*

"When you receive good news you want to share it. Recently, one of my top clients went on and on with praise about how much his Make Your Paycheck Last money management system has enabled him to better plan his family's income... he said he'd be lost without it."
—*Certified Financial Planner, New York*

"I have read just about every book on family financial planning. However, none come close to Make Your Paycheck

Last. It is by far the best, most complete guide I've read on the subject."

—Financial services firm, California

"We give this a four-star value rating. Don't pass it up."

—Editor, Washington

"I have made strong recommendations to several clients to adopt your program."

—Financial consultant, Colorado

"In all my research, I have never seen a more descriptive, easy-to-follow plan. I wish I would have had your book 10 years ago."

—Financial consultant, Wisconsin

"The book is concise and clear, and the support materials are what has been missing in other approaches to helping the lay person do a better job with personal finances."
—Educator, Colorado

"My wife and I sat up last night until 2 a.m. discussing our goals...what an education!

—Ph.D., Wisconsin

"Make Your Paycheck Last gets people to think about things they want out of their life... not just taking things as they come."

—Accountant, Wisconsin

ACKNOWLEDGEMENTS

I would like to thank all the bankers, lawyers, CPAs, consultants, brokers, insurance agents and accountants I consulted for motivating me to develop a simpler method, one that you don't need a Ph.D. to use or 50 hours a day to implement. In other words, a simple financial planning method that will work for *you*.

I would like to thank my wife, Sandy, for helping me develop the method you're about to discover, and for joining me on our own journey to a better financial life.

And I thank Ron Fry and the staff at Career Press for publishing this new edition of *Make Your Paycheck Last* so it can help *you*.

PREFACE

Many years ago, as a newly hired airline copilot, I asked seasoned captains for their financial advice. What I heard didn't make sense. Why were so many of these well-paid pilots broke nearly every pay day? They earned a lot of money, but didn't have any plan or goals...or savings. They wanted "it" all—even though none of them were particularly sure what "it" was or how to attain "it". And, of course, they wanted it all *right now*.

So, I started talking to the professional money people—the accountants, attorneys, CPAs, bankers, financial planners and various other counselors. They didn't seem to have any of the *simple* answers I was really looking for. All I found were complicated, unrealistic theories.

So my wife, Sandy, and I started to develop our own workable system. Where did we start? That was easy—we wrote down what we wanted... *everything* we wanted, from the stuff we needed tomorrow to the big dreams far (we thought) in the future. These became our goals, or the "reasons" we were willing to change whatever needed to change for us to get to where we wanted our lives to go. Goals like a home in the country, a vacation and getting out of debt. Yep, goals just like yours.

Next we decided what we wanted *first*. We didn't always agree on which came first, but we found that talking over coffee at our kitchen table was all it required. Actually, going out to our favorite restaurant worked best because we were both on neutral ground. Besides, everyone has a better outlook when they don't have to fix the meal or wash the dishes.

Once we developed this simple and easy system and put it into practice, it was a surprisingly short time before we took a ski vacation in Europe, built our home in the country, and began making investments... and we were getting out of debt, to boot. Best of all, financially it made us an unbeatable couple. We're not rich, but we'll never be out of control of our own finances again. Having done it, I'm here to tell you that you can do it too...and I'll show you how.

Hundreds of thousands of people are on my plan now—we've sold more than 500,000 copies of the first edition of this book. So, again, do not fear—if it's worked for all of them, it has to work for you.

What's so different that we had to make this a "second edition"? Well, I've changed some words I wrote a while back—we all get better at some things as we get older—updated all the numbers, reworked some of the illustrations and charts, and changed some of the questions (and answers) in

Chapter 5 to reflect the many thousands of letters I've received over the years. So this new edition of *Make Your Paycheck Last* is as complete and up-to-date as I can make it. And it's completely redesigned to be easier to read and easier to use. But the "meat" of this book—the *method* of how to *Make Your Paycheck Last*—is the same one I've been using for 17 years. The same one that will work for you.

What else do you need besides this book (and maybe a pencil and some paper)? Nothing. However (just one small "but," I promise), a number of people told us they didn't want to have to make the forms necessary to keep track of their planning and spending. So we produced a companion workbook that contains all the charts you need to implement this financial planning method immediately.

This workbook really gets you going and keeps you organized. You'll be able to see your total financial situation at a glance as far as a full year into your future. To thank you for purchasing this book, we have included a special discount coupon so you can receive your own copy of the workbook at a special price.

You can do it! Start with Chapter 1, and stick to it!

Harold Moe

INTRODUCTION

Where To Start

Everyone feels a sense of pride and satisfaction when they make a positive effort to confront a problem. Resolving to change the way you deal with your personal finances is no exception. It's taking that first step—making the commitment to *take control*—that makes you feel good.

So congratulations! You *should* feel good. Because 90 percent of your friends and neighbors know very little about money management, to say nothing about actually *doing* something about it. And 80 percent of Americans have never had a savings account. *Only 10 percent* of our total population controls how they spend their money.

That's what I am going to show you in this book, in the same language you learned in high school, so you can *immediately* take control and start reaching your dreams.

As a financial consultant I have met many people who, like you, have recognized the importance of getting control of their money. *Recognizing* the overwhelming importance of that control—realizing that it is the basis for *any* financial plan, no matter how simple or complicated—

is the first step to getting the most out of your income and learning *how* to control it to get what you want from your work efforts.

Over the years I have introduced personal financial plans to men and women of every background. People just like you, all with the same objective—to get a better grip on their money. In this book, I will introduce you to the same type of financial plan, at a much lower cost. Granted, I'm not sitting at your kitchen table, your bills stacked around us, helping you figure it all out...at a nice hourly fee. And that's why this book is such a good deal for you—it's still the same plan, only quieter.

What will we be talking about in this book? Well, we begin right where you are. Most people have some information to start with, while others are just now realizing they should (or must) do something to get better control of their money.

You may have noticed that I call my method a plan and not a budget. There's a very good reason for that. A budget is a monthly system that says you have so much money to spend on food, so much money for entertainment, so much for rent, and so on. Many people put different amounts of cash in envelopes marked "food," "entertainment," "rent," etc. That's one way to budget, and it works. However, it tends to be time-limited, lasting only a specific length of time—while you're in college, during a financial crisis, military service, or the first (or last) years of marriage. The numerous steps required to maintain this type of budget is the principal reason it tends to be so limited.

At one time or another, most people I have worked with used this "self-sealing envelope" budget.

Other people have used a book to record each dollar that gets spent. I used this system when I was in school. In recording everything I was spending, I really was not budgeting. I was recording dollar amounts *after* we parted company. Likewise, using either method I have described does not tell me how much money I will need in six months, or whether I will be able to save that amount while continuing my present rate of spending. These methods only tell me how much money I have to spend. When it's gone...that's it until next pay day!

Nevertheless, any method you have already been using to account for your monthly spending is valuable. You will be putting that information to good use in the next two chapters.

What if you don't have any records or past budgeting experience? That's OK. You may very well do *better* since you haven't experienced "pay day trauma," which results in poor self-control and questionable spending practices.

What considerations should be given to a good financial plan? If you're like most people, you'll want your plan not only to record what you're spending, but also provide information so you can:

1. **Accurately determine how much income you will need** to meet obligations 6 or even 12 months from now. At the same time, you will want to measure your progress each month (and pat yourself on the back as your monthly progress proves to be right on target).

2. **Actively plan for those things you would someday like.** That's right! *Actively* do something today to bring you closer to where you want to be tomorrow.

3. **Have all your monthly obligations clearly displayed right in front of you.** There are some real benefits to doing this. Most people find they are in better financial shape than they had feared. If your fears are confirmed, you now have the means to recognize their cause.

4. Have a system that quickly shows **where you have the spending control you want.** Likewise, a system that will show *when* and *where* spending is getting out of hand.

5. Have a plan that will **reward you each month in extra, real money** (what I call a

surplus) as you continue to use it. To say nothing about that terrific feeling of being a winner!

6. Have a plan that **doesn't require all your free time to manage.** Once you begin using this plan, you will need no more than one hour each month. That's all...60 minutes a month! That's not much. If you use more time, it's probably because you are watching TV while you do it, or, better yet, patting yourself on the back for a job well done. Just 15 minutes each week. Isn't having control of your spending worth that small amount of time? Of course it is!

One last thought before we begin. This system works 100 percent of the time for 99 percent of the people that are on my program. Why? Because I move along one step at a time, never charging ahead until each step is complete. Since I am not able to be with you, it is very important for *you* to keep pace, not jump ahead. There is no time limit, nor any special reward for getting to the end of the book faster than your spouse! I tested this (book) method and got the same great results...as long as everyone proceeded step-by-step. If you will do that, it's 99 percent certain you will have the control you want over your money. As a bonus, you'll have that great feeling of confidence and satisfaction that comes from taking charge of your paycheck.

Ready? Here we go: Find three sheets of paper, a pencil and clear the kitchen table so we can get started.

Remember: Your "someday" is *today*.

TABLE OF CONTENTS

CHAPTER 1
LET'S SET SOME GOALS

Seventeen years ago, my wife Sandy and I sat down at our kitchen table and asked ourselves: "Where are we really going?" "What do we really want?" "How do we intend to get there?" Each week we had barely enough money to last until the next paycheck. Sometimes not even barely. We didn't have money in the bank...or anywhere else for that matter. We knew we should be saving—how could we buy a house without a down payment?—and we'd tried a couple of times. But something always seemed to eat up those dollars before we even got a chance to set them aside.

Our car—a Chevy Impala with a crumpled fender that used a quart of transmission fluid a week—needed major surgery. We were making payments to Sears on our stove and refrigerator. There were a dozen or two other things we needed (or wanted), and our daughter was soon to be a reality.

There was always something important to buy. Just enough to buy it. Nothing left for anything else.

It was about that time that I stumbled on a simple financial truth: "It's not what you make that counts; it's what you *do* with what you make." Or, as I would put it now: "Plan ahead to get ahead."

Sandy and I took that advice. In one short (but certainly not easy) year, we moved into our first home. Best of all, our mortgage was our only debt.

How did we manage to change our financial picture in such a short time? In a word, we made buying a home our number one priority, instead of spending all our money on those "other" things that kept us from getting it a year or two earlier.

What "other" things? Oh, you know—those "never-to-be-repeated, once-in-a-lifetime, red-hot deals" that simply kept us from focusing on something we really wanted and were capable of achieving.

Let's play 20 questions

Carefully answer these questions to get a better feel for how it works:

1. How do you think a financial plan can help you? Why are you reading this book? What do you expect it to do for you?

2. Why do you go to work everyday? What's it going to get you in 10 years? Where do you want to *be* in 10 years?

3. What are the plans you talk about only to yourself...or your best friend...or your spouse?

Let your mind go jogging for a few minutes and listen to what it comes up with. These ideas are full of promise and hope. It doesn't matter if it's a little thing like a new coat or repainting the living room, or a big deal like a vacation retreat or a new car or college for the kids. What is important is that it's important to *you*!

Remember the times you've said, "Sometime, wouldn't it be great to...?" or "Someday I'm going to...?" I'm sure you can fill in the blanks many times over.

One question I've found to be a real idea-starter in my own counseling sessions is, "What would you choose to do with your time, if it were yours?"

Now that you've asked all these questions and written down a page or two of answers, what does this exercise mean? Simply that if what you have described can be acknowledged as realistic goals, it's *99-percent certain* that you can achieve them.

What does all this have to do with a financial plan? Plenty, since you want to take control of your financial future. After all, there is nothing wrong with getting bills paid. But the bigger question is, how did you get there in the first place and why? Why not get your finances in order and then keep things going in your chosen direction? After all, the foundation for good financial planning has nothing to do with money. It has to do with setting goals and working out a method to attain them. (That's right, the method included in this book.)

The illustration on the next page will be helpful in understanding how goal-setting works. Take a moment to study it.

I want, I need, I wish...

How do you get started on the road to achieving your goals (or, if you prefer, your hopes, plans or expectations)? First and foremost: *Write them down*. Make a written description of what you want or where you want your life to go.

And realize that timing is a factor, if not *the* factor. It's too late to begin worrying about your retirement income once you're dressed for your 65th birthday party. And your child's high school graduation is not a good time to wonder where his or her college money is going to come from.

Wishing will never make any type of dream home a reality, nor is the day the pink slip lands on your (former) desk a time to resolve to stop living from paycheck to paycheck.

Goals come in three "sizes": long-term, medium and short-term.

Long-term goals are those that will be realized in 15 to 20 years. For some of you, that's when the kids will all be in college or on their own. For others, it could be when you start your own business or retire from it. Depending on how young you are now, this may mean planning for when you're 40, 55 or 70. How old you are now—and how old you'll be when your long-term goals fall into (or out of) place—doesn't really matter. *Whatever* long-term goals you have, you must take action today to realize your tomorrow...even a small action, like defining where you want to be 20 years from now.

Medium goals are those you hope to achieve in about 5 years. Some examples: new furniture, a camper van, a vacation to Europe, the down payment on that new home or vacation retreat, or getting your debts (finally!) paid off. Interestingly, medium goals are the easiest for many people to achieve. The reason will become clear as you begin using your financial plan.

Short-term goals are those you hope to realize in the next 12 months or so. A short-term goal could be a new living room chair, paying off a charge account or siding the house. There was a time—actually, only a generation ago—when a short-term goal was thought to be 5 or 10 years down the road. Today the pace of society has accelerated to the point that to want *any*thing is to want it *now*. Even if getting it jeopardizes other plans for the next several years.

Unrealistic short-term expectations cause most financial crises that arise in the course of our everyday lives. The first danger signs are statements like:

- "I really do need that today."

- "I suppose it really wouldn't pay to fix up the old one."

- "It's so pretty!"
- "This is a once-in-a-lifetime chance."
- "You only go around once."
- "I owe it to myself."
- "I know I can't afford it, but..."
- "Why not?"
- "I simply must have that...now!"

Whenever you start thinking this sort of self-defeating bunk, take two aspirin and go straight to bed. Stay there until the urge passes.

How do you determine if a goal is realistic? No problem. Your goals will reveal themselves when they are tested with the financial plan you will develop in the next two chapters.

Your goals are important. They give you purpose and direction. Goals enable you to identify what you want and the direction you would like your life to go. They are the most important part of any sound financial plan. In a family situation, goals unify effort, since everyone knows the objective and can pull together.

If you do nothing today to bring yourself closer to where you want to be tomorrow, tomorrow will still come, whether you're ready or not. Each of us is different, but we each have just 24 hours in our day. The president has the same 24 hours a

day as you or I. No more, no less. It's what you
do with what you have that's important. What you
don't have is not important. Without a goal, no
budget or financial plan can possible work.
Without a goal, there is nothing to come true.

Let's make a list

Take one sheet of paper and write "Long-Term
Goals" at the top. If you're married, your spouse
should make a separate list. Do your own writing,
and don't compare lists until you have completed
this entire step. List your long-term goals from "1"
through "10." Many of you will be lucky to come
up with three or four long-term goals. However, do
not *exceed* 10. By limiting yourself in this way, you
won't become overwhelmed. (It's like working
around the house on a weekend. If you have three
or four projects to get done, they can be completed in time for lunch. If you find yourself facing a
dozen tasks, you won't even complete one—you
become so overwhelmed that you simply collapse
on the couch before you even get started.)

On a second sheet of paper, make a list of your
medium goals. (Again, spouses do separate lists,
please!) What would you like to accomplish within the next five years? Take your time and let your
mind wander. Again, limit yourself to a list of not
more than 10 goals (seven or eight is average).

Finally, on a third sheet, list those objectives you want to achieve in the next year. Again, limit yourself to the 10 most important goals. Usually 15 or 20 ideas will come to mind. Save the extra 5 or 10 and make them next year's goals. Only the 10 hottest ones for now!

Look over your lists one more time. Once you are satisfied with your selections, compare your lists with your spouse's. Major important rule: Don't criticize your spouse's list. Accept it as being what your spouse really feels (just as you expect him or her to accept your lists).

It is now time to combine the two long-term goal lists into one. Take turns adding one item from each list until you total 10 *as a couple*. Do the same with the medium and short-term lists.

If, during the next few days, you think it over and want to change a goal, do so. But only change the ones *you* contributed to the joint list, unless your spouse agrees to change one of his or hers.

Remember your goals! That is so important. Your goals are the most important ingredient for the success of your financial plan. I know people who memorize them. Others post them where the bills are paid or tack them on the bathroom mirror or up on the refrigerator. Whatever works for you is fine.

An example, like a picture, is worth a thousand words. In this case, the story of Bill and Mary

Stevenson can illustrate what I have just talked about. Bill and Mary's story is real. I have changed their names only because it seemed like the right thing to do.

Bill is a teacher and brings home $1,656 per month. Mary works part-time at her father's flower shop. Their story is the example we will follow throughout this book in setting up your own financial plan. Their income and expenses may appear a little low to you—I am using their initial plan, which now is several years old. However, even though the numbers may differ from yours, the plan is valid as an example because the percentages remain the same. In other words, if their car payment appears to be half what yours is, the Stevenson's income is probably half as much also. The point here is that by using their actual plan, regardless of the dollar amounts (due to a few years of inflation), you will have a much better chance to relate.

On the next page you will see a reprint of what the Stevenson's arrived at after combining their goal lists. Take the time to thoroughly review their lists.

Bill and Mary spent some time on these lists. They talked about each goal and both felt satisfied with them. In a year, or less, they will sit down to review their lists and evaluate their progress. At that time, they may make changes to

SHORT TERM GOALS — 12 months

1. Pay off Visa	$1050.00
2. End surprise bills - Insurance, Medical, etc.	
3. Car Cassette Player	210.00
4. Develop a closer relationship as a couple	
5. Get spending under control	
6. Hide-A-Bed for living room	300.00
7. Refinishing sander	60.00
8. X-country Skis (Mary)	125.00
9. Winterize car	200.00
10. Refinish dining room table	
	$1945.00

MEDIUM TERM GOALS - 5 years

1. Honda motorcycle	$ 950.00
2. Financial security from strikes and medical emergencies	2000.00
3. Down payment on home	4000.00
4. Have baby	1000.00
5. New car down payment	600.00
6. Replace bedroom set	800.00
7. Color TV	400.00
	$9750.00

LONG TERM GOALS - 15 years

1. Be established in university level education	
2. Vacation to England	$5000.00
ILLUSTRATION 2	**$5000.00**

and growing. Priorities and goals change just as we change as individuals.

Besides dating their lists, whenever a dollar value could be assigned, they made a ball-park guess.

Keys to successful goal-setting

1. When making goal lists, start with your long-term goals first.

2. Your goal lists should be kept in a handy place for frequent reference and encouragement.

3. If you are married, work together and agree that your goals are worthy of everyone involved.

4. Each year our lives change; so will some goals. Remain as flexible as possible.

5. Year after year, continue to save your goal lists. They are your best measure of progress.

6. Remember your goals. It's not just a matter of priority—the success of your financial plan depends on it.

Congratulations again! Your have already completed the most difficult part of constructing your financial plan. Armed with your three goal lists, let's continue to Chapter 2.

CHAPTER 2

LAYING OUT YOUR FINANCIAL PLAN

I t's already time to start laying out your financial plan, which is divided into four sections that we will call "Savings," "Obligations," "Net Income" and "Surplus." As you'll see from the ongoing example of the Stevensons, the form you need to use to construct your plan is relatively simple to make. (If you have or want to purchase the companion workbook, you'll find four full financial plan forms already laid out for you.)

Especially the first time around, your financial plan will go through changes and adjustments, so plan on using one sheet to "draft" your plan and another to finalize it in more legible form.

Let's begin with the section titled "Obligations." These are the ***monthly*** payments to the butcher, the baker, the candlestick-maker and anyone else. The better your record-keeping—check registers, budget records, expense receipts and reports, etc.—the easier filling out this section month-by-month will be.

Projecting your spending

To illustrate how this section is completed, follow along with the Stevenson's example on pp. 18 & 19. Bill and Mary have listed all the areas where they spend money each month.

Rent is self-explanatory. (If you are a homeowner, Mortgage would be the appropriate title for your entry.) The Stevensons live in a one-bedroom, unfurnished apartment. Their $405 monthly rent is written in small numbers at the top-right corner of the square to the right of the Rent title. This amount is really a projection of what Bill and Mary *plan* to spend. After they write their rent check, they will enter the actual amount they spent in large numbers below this projection (but still in the same square on the form). See pp. 18 & 19 for their completed financial plan for this month.

Notice also, the Stevenson's didn't start their plan until February, so January entries were left blank.

Electric company. The Stevenson's are on the budget plan and project a cost of $45 each month for light and electric heat. Budget plans are a great help in financial planning. If you are unable to subscribe to such a plan (they go by several names), use past receipts to estimate seasonal fluctuations. Add 10 percent to your last year's cost for an inflation factor, or your utility company can give you an accurate idea of what to expect this year. Many heating oil companies also offer budget plans. It's worth asking about.

Telephone bills are directly controlled by you. When there is a need to reduce spending, your phone is a good place to start. Sending a postcard or letter is an easy way to put you back on firm financial ground without upsetting your standard of living.

Make Your Paycheck Last

FINANCIAL PLAN

SAVINGS

REAL & PROJECTED

YEAR	JAN	FEB	MAR	APR	MAY	JUN	JUL	AUG	SEPT	OCT	NOV	DEC
CREDIT UNION		248 -	248 -	248 -	248 -	248 -						
STATE BANK		75 -	75 -	75 -	75 -	75 -						
TOTAL SAVINGS		323 -	323 -	323 -	323 -	323 -						

OBLIGATIONS

	JAN	FEB	MAR	APR	MAY	JUN	JUL	AUG	SEPT	OCT	NOV	DEC
RENT		905 -	905 -	905 -	905 -	905 -						
ELECTRIC COMPANY		45 -	45 -	45 -	45 -	45 -						
TELEPHONE		33 -	33 -	33 -	33 -	33 -						
GIFTS AND CONTRIBUTIONS		16 -	16 -	16 -	16 -	16 -						
HOUSEHOLD		440 -	440 -	440 -	440 -	440 -						
CAR PAYMENT		60 -	60 -	60 -	60 -	60 -			58 -			
STEREO PAYMENT		37.50	37.50	37.50	37.50	37.50			26 -			
CHARGE PAYMENT VISA SEARS CITGO		203.50	203.50	203.50	203.50	203.50						
SCHOOL EXPENSE -BILL		80 -	80 -	80 -	80 -	80 -						
RECREATION AND ENTERTAINMENT		50 -	50 -	50 -	50 -	50 -						
MISC		65 -	65 -	65 -	65 -	65 -						

Laying out your financial plan

TOTAL OBLIGATIONS	1758-	1758-	1758-	1758-	1758-					

NET INCOME

BILL	1656-	1656-	1656-	1656-	1656-		1677-			
MARY	118-	118-	118-	118-	118-			148-	148-	148-
TOTAL INCOME	1774-	1774-	1774-	1774-	1774-					

SURPLUS

	16-	16-	16-	16-	16-					

Most telephone companies offer a call-pack promotion. Where considerable long-distance calling is necessary, this service can reduce charges up to about 50 percent.

Gifts and contributions are charitable or religious donations made on a more or less regular basis.

Household. Mary plans and buys the groceries and household supplies. The projected $440 also includes an amount for Mary to spend as she sees fit. More about this category later.

Car payment is a coupon-type installment payment. Each coupon book payment should be listed separately. Also, as you can see in the example, their car will be paid off in October of this year.

Stereo. The stereo package is another coupon payment that will end in September.

Charge payment. One short-term goal Bill and Mary have is to pay off their Visa card this year. If you haven't taken the time, read over their goal lists in Chapter 1. I will be making several references to it in this section.

They also have Sears and Citgo credit cards. Both have mutually agreed to discontinue using their Visa and Sears cards until they are paid off.

Since Bill and Mary get gas at their neighborhood Citgo station, they feel a credit card is more convenient than cash. The $203.50 projected payment is computed this way: Bill placed paying Visa ($1,050) as his first short-term goal. Dividing this amount equally over twelve months means that $87.50 per month will pay off the total due in one year. Sears gets $40. Both Visa and Sears payments are greater than the required minimum payment. The Stevensons pay their Citgo bill, which averages $76, in full each month. Add it all up—$203.50 a month.

Looks good, and they have met their first short-term goal as a bonus!

School expenses. Bill uses this money to buy some meals at school, as well as other school-related expenses. He feels the $80 projection will leave something for him to spend as he sees fit.

Entertainment can be a tough cookie! Originally Bill and Mary actually spent $195 per month on their entertainment. From the first draft of their financial plan, it was clear there just wasn't enough cash to go around. After reviewing their goals and monthly obligations, they felt entertainment was their best candidate for adjustment.

Instead of eating out each week, they've planned for twice a month. If there is any money left in "Surplus," they may eat out more.

Entertainment was very important to Bill and Mary. Eating out, movies and plays were a large part of their lifestyle, After they considered their goals, they found that entertainment was one of the biggest contributing factors to their somewhat delicate financial condition.

Bill and Mary also found a new word: recreation, which costs a lot less than entertainment! Bike riding, tennis, walks in the park, and the municipal pool now supplement entertainment to help keep their costs in line. Additionally, the Stevensons found that recreation, as a couple, helps realize their fourth short-term goal.

Miscellaneous is a catchall area for those unanticipated expenses. All financial plans should include this heading. Bill and Mary include subscriptions and occasional drug store prescriptions in this category.

Note: If any single item consistently finds its way into Miscellaneous, consider adding a separate entry title for it.

Other monthly obligation titles you may need to add: Childcare, Utilities, Tuition, Auto Expense, Laundry, Medical/Dental, Business Expense, Allowances, Support, Cleaning/Maintenance, Car Pool, Clothing.

Now that you've seen how it's done, make up your own form and list your monthly obligations on your own financial plan. If you aren't sure about a particular item and have no records to consult, estimate as best you can. You can always adjust as you proceed.

If you don't have a checking account, open one. It will provide an excellent (and easy-to-maintain) record of money spent. Also, a checking account provides a reliable means of controlling spending as well as valuable income tax documentation.

Plus it is a demonstrated fact that using a checking account is more economical and clearly more accurate than paying cash.

Deposit all income into your checking account, and make all payments from it (wherever possible). If you're married, two checking accounts will work even better.

Bill and Mary use two accounts. The first (or primary account) is used for everything but Mary's household expenses—all income is deposited into it, and all monthly bills and savings are paid from this account. A check is written to Mary for $440 to cover her monthly household expenses, which she then deposits into her own checking account.

There are several benefits to this arrangement. First, Mary is able to plan and control her spending better than if she has a large amount of cash around.

Second, a separate checking account gives Mary a greater sense of pride in that she has her own money to spend. As long as she meets her obligation to household spending—that is, as long as she doesn't spend more than has been allotted—she is never called to account for how she spends this money. This is also true for Bill and the area of his personal spending.

Finally, when Bill and Mary evaluate their financial plan, they will have a much more accurate record to justify any needed changes in household spending.

In a family situation, the purchasing of the household supplies, groceries, clothes and related items tends to fall to one person. These expenses will require a greater number of purchases and will be easier to manage with the second checking account.

However, in a situation where one spouse has proven to be unable to exercise the necessary spending control, it is best to use only one checking account.

Let there be crises

Now, let's see how two *savings* accounts can work for you. Each year everyone has payments that surprise and frustrate their best-laid plan. Insurance payments head the "there has got to be a better way to handle this" list. There is! By saving a little each month, there will be money to make those payments that appear at the most inconvenient intervals.

Examples of these bills: taxes, insurance, bank note payments, auto repairs, heating oil (not on a budget plan), annual school tuition, vacation money, health club or other membership dues, etc. These are all bills we *know* will arrive, but we may not know *when*...or that so many will seem to arrive so often. I have come to call these the "Not-So-Monthly Obligations." Once you have a handle on them, they aren't nearly so difficult to work with. How do you figure out how much to save? The illustration below should put it into perspective.

BEFORE SAVINGS: AFTER SAVINGS:

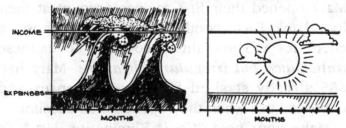

BY SAVING MONTHLY, YOU WILL ELIMINATE THOSE FINANCIAL CRISIS TIMES!

When the Stevensons prepared their list of "Not-So-Monthly Obligations" (or, if you prefer, their "Crisis Elimination List"), they included the dollar amount, obligation and the month the bill arrived.

After combining their receipts, recollections and notes, the Stevensons' list looked like this:

Crisis Elimination List

$120	Contribution to teachers group medical plan	(Feb.)
210	Auto insurance	(Apr.)
148	Life insurance (Bill)	(Apr.)
131	Life insurance (Mary)	(June)
80	Dentist	(Aug.)
200	Winterize car (short-term goal)	(Oct.)
889		

The total—$889—is divided into 12 monthly payments of $75 (rounding off high). Bill and Mary opened their first savings account at their local bank. Each month Bill writes and deposits a check for $75 into this account to cover these *anticipated but irregular obligations*. Mary had $85 already stashed for these expenses and deposited this when they opened their account.

Make your own "Crisis Elimination List." To help your short-term savings program, use the chart on the next page to organize your payments. Start with the examples we used at the start of this discussion. Finally, review your short-term goal list.

Your Crisis Elimination List

Amount	Obligation	Month due

1. _____

2. _____

3. _____

4. _____

5. _____

6. _____

7. _____

8. _____

9. _____

$_____ divided by 12 (months)

= $_____ saved each month
in your short-term savings account
to eliminate the crisis times!

Don't list small things like magazine subscriptions, since these are easier to pay out of miscellaneous funds ("Obligations" section). Notice that the Stevensons chose to put their dentist on their list. You may find it easier to make that payment out of "Obligations" and not your short-term savings. Consider your situation and decide what will work easiest for you.

Credit unions and most banks now offer interest on many checking accounts—these accounts are ideal when planning your Crisis Elimination List in that you will receive the same interest as a passbook-type savings account. But, you can write the necessary checks at home, saving the time and expense of a trip to the bank to make your withdrawal.

Turn back to Bill's and Mary's original financial plan on pp. 18 & 19 and you'll note that they entered $75 as the amount projected to be saved in this account each month.

You can see how this savings plan can smooth out the crises that tend to strike every few months.

Your second savings account should be used to provide opportunity. It will bring you, each month, one step closer to where you want to be tomorrow. To clarify how this is accomplished, follow along as the Stevensons compute their *long-term savings plan*.

On their goal lists, the Stevensons assigned a dollar cost to all the goals they could. (For convenience, I have included another copy of their goal list on the next page.) Bill and Mary included paying off their Visa account in their monthly obliga-

SHORT TERM GOALS — 12 months

DONE 1. Pay off Visa	$ 1050.00
DONE 2. End surprise bills - Insurance, Medical, etc.	
3. Car Cassette Player	210.00
4. Develop a closer relationship as a couple	
5. Get spending under control	
6. Hide-A-Bed for living room	300.00
7. Refinishing sander	60.00
8. X-Country Skis (Mary)	125.00
DONE 9. Winterize car	200.00
10. Refinish dining room table	
	$1945.00

MEDIUM TERM GOALS — 5 years

1. Honda motorcycle	$ 950.00
2. Financial security from strikes and medical emergencies	2000.00
3. Down payment on home	4000.00
4. Have baby	1000.00
5. New car down payment	600.00
6. Replace bedroom set	800.00
7. Color TV	400.00
	$9750.00

LONG TERM GOALS — 15 years

1. Be established in university level education	
2. Vacation to England	$5000.00
	$5000.00

tions. The winterization of their car and surprise bills were included in their short-term savings account. Since three of their 10 short-term goals are already accounted for elsewhere, here's how all their remaining goals add up:

$695   The total remaining short-term goals. It would require $58 per month ($695 divided by 12) for one year to realize these remaining goals.

$9,750   The total medium goals, which require $162 per month ($9,750 divided by 60 months) for five years to achieve.

$5,000   Total long-term goals, which require $28 per month ($5,000 divided by 180 months) for 15 years to realize.

Add these monthly obligations together:

Short-term goals	=	$ 58 per month
Medium goals	=	162 per month
Long-term goals	=	28 per month
Total		$248 per month

On their financial plan, Bill and Mary entered a projection of $248 in small numbers across from the savings titled Credit union. By saving this amount each month, the Stevensons will have the money necessary to meet each of the monetary goals they have set for themselves.

And these totals do not reflect the interest they will receive on this money while it is in their savings account...a definite bonus!

Another bonus is the fact that their new savings and checking accounts have given the Stevensons a sound credit base. It will do the same for you.

Do you see the importance of two savings accounts? The first, a **short-term account**, is used to smooth out the roughness of the "Not-So-Monthly Obligations." The second, a **long-term account**, will make your future goals possible. Your checking account provides organization and control, but it's a consistent savings program that will enable you to have the wherewithal to take advantage of opportunity. Do not overlook the absolute importance of a consistent, determined savings program.

Your turn: Complete the savings portions of your financial plan. Use the forms on the following pages and enter your projections as the Stevensons did. These totals will be combined to complete your long-term savings projections.

Refer back to your goal lists and include all remaining short-term goals on the following chart, with a dollar amount for each:

Dollar amount   Short-term goal

1. _____   _____

2. _____   _____

3. _____   _____

4. _____   _____

5. _____   _____

6. _____   _____

7. _____   _____

8. _____   _____

9. _____   _____

10. _____   _____

$ _____   Total amount divided by
12 (months) =

$ _____

Refer back to your goal lists and include all remaining medium goals on the following chart, with a dollar amount for each:

	Dollar amount	Medium goal
1.	_____	_____
2.	_____	_____
3.	_____	_____
4.	_____	_____
5.	_____	_____
6.	_____	_____
7.	_____	_____
8.	_____	_____
9.	_____	_____
10.	_____	_____

$ _____ Total amount divided by
60 (months) =

$ _____

Refer back to your goal lists and include all remaining long-term goals on the following chart, with a dollar amount for each:

	Dollar amount	Long-term goal
1.	_____	_____
2.	_____	_____
3.	_____	_____
4.	_____	_____
5.	_____	_____
6.	_____	_____
7.	_____	_____
8.	_____	_____
9.	_____	_____
10.	_____	_____

$ _____ Total amount divided by 180 (months) =

$ _____

Now add the three totals together:

Short-term goals = $ _____ per month
Medium goals = $ _____ per month
Long-term goals = $ _____ per month

Total $ _____ per month

This is the amount you must deposit each month into your long-term savings (your "opportunity") account to meet all your goals. Enter this amount in the appropriate square of the "Savings" section of your financial plan. Believe it or not, you're just one step away from *completing* your plan!

Before we get there, let's go back and look at the Stevensons' example one more time. Look back at their original financial plan (pp. 18 & 19) and you'll note they added all the various columns: They have a total for savings at the bottom of the column—$323— and for obligations—$1,758. **Total your own savings and obligations projections.**

Now let's turn to the "Net Income" section. Net income is the amount of money you actually bring home (yes, that's "take-home" pay). Bill brings home $1,656, Mary adds another $118, for a total of $1,774 per month. This amount is entered at the bottom of the "Income" column of the Stevensons' projection. In September, Bill expects to get a raise—he has indicated it in the September income column. Mary works one more day a week in October, November, and December. This increase is also included in their projections.

Enter your own income projections. Be sure to indicate any changes—up or down—you expect throughout the year. (This is also true when entering projections for savings and monthly obligations.)

We're now ready to look at the "bottom line" (now you know where they get that term), which I'll call "Surplus." What's is it? The simplest way to express it: Subtract total "Obligations" from total "Income." What's left is "Surplus." Or, to look at it another way: To this point, you have provided for all your monthly obligations, you have saved for those not-so-monthly obligations, and you have saved for the future. Whatever is left is surplus money.

What does a hard-working manager of personal finance do with a surplus? Write yourself a check for a job well done!

Over the years, Sandy and I have used our monthly surplus for a canoe, a chain saw, a horse, increased savings and extra dinners out. Remember: The harder you work your financial plan, the more surplus you will have.

It is important to take any surplus money out of your checking account so that it doesn't accumulate. There seems to be a natural tendency to want to let surplus money accumulate for some future moment. Hopefully, you will soon see why this is not a good idea.

Bill and Mary always leave $25 in their account to prevent an overdraft. This is a good idea. In reality, this $25 buffer is a "zero balance" and is treated as such. When this balance is reached, no more money is spent.

To see this more clearly, let's assume Bill and Mary let their surplus accumulate to, say, $45. With their $70 checking account balance ($45 surplus and $25 buffer = $70), they decide to spend $50 on something or other. Suddenly, their financial plan is in the red by $5, even though their checking account shows a balance of $20.

Not good.

By removing surplus money from your checking account, you're actually balancing your checkbook with your financial plan. That's important.

It's a good idea to have a buffer. And to remove any surplus above that buffer before it begins to accumulate. I'll show you how in Chapter 3.

Stop! Before going on, be certain you do the following:

1. Complete your financial plan, with projections for (at least) the first six months.
2. Open one or two checking accounts.
3. Open two savings accounts.

If your just-completed financial plan projections show a loss of more than $30 (a negative surplus), go directly to Chapter 4. Do not pass "Go"! Do not refill your coffee cup.

If your financial plan projections show a surplus, take a break and I'll see you in Chapter 3.

CHAPTER 3

60 MINUTES OF KEEPING UP.

In this chapter, we'll discuss everything necessary to keep your financial plan up to date, month after month. Just please note how surprisingly little "everything" is!

Maintaining your financial plan is nothing more than entering the amount of money actually spent in each category of "Obligations" and "Savings." There are two ways to do this: The first is simple; the second merely easy.

The first method is used when *one* check is written per obligation each month. I prefer to use this method just to familiarize you with the simplicity of keeping your plan up to date, since I don't feel it's realistic for most of you. (However, if you are single or retired and write no more than one check per month in each category of obligation, this method would be the easiest for you to use.)

Your checkbook provides a means of recording all the checks you write, either in the form of a copy of your check or a check register. Either way, starting with the first check of the month, enter the actual check amount under your projection for each obligation on your financial plan.

After all checks have been entered, total the monthly column. Enter this total under your projection for "Total Obligations."

Lastly, subtract "Total Obligations" from "Net Income." The remainder is your "Surplus."

Simple? Yes!

More than likely, you will be writing *several* checks in the categories of Miscellaneous, Charge Payments, Entertainment and Household (especially if you decide not to use a second checking account for this area).

The second method is used to simplify updating your financial plan when more than one check is written in any category each month. This method offers the advantage of being able to see where, when and why checks are written (control) and, though it takes a little longer, it's actually easier.

Let me illustrate. Bill and Mary ended the month of February by writing 19 checks. The following page is a reproduction of their check register.

Using a simple form I've called a "Financial Plan Worksheet," Bill and Mary transferred the information from their check register to an easier-to-use spreadsheet (see p. 43.) First, they titled each column according to the Obligation entries they had on their financial plan. Then, from their check register, they entered each check by number and description (with the dollar amount entered in the appropriate column).

After all the checks were entered, each column was totaled, giving them the actual dollars spent in each category.

These actual totals are then entered on the financial plan (as I've already done for you on the example on pp. 44 & 45).

With the actual amounts for "Savings" and "Obligations" entered, all that remains is to add the monthly column. That will give the actual

Make Your Paycheck Last

RECORD ALL CHARGES OR CREDITS THAT AFFECT YOUR ACCOUNT

NUMBER	DATE	DESCRIPTION OF TRANSACTION	PAYMENT/DEBIT (-)	√ T	FEE (IF ANY) (-)	DEPOSIT/CREDIT (+)	BALANCE
							25 00
	2/1	Deposit (Bill)				828 00	853 00
101	2/1	Rent	405 00				
102	2/1	Credit Union	248 00				200 00
	2/5	Deposit (Mary)				118 00	318 00
103	2/5	Second Finance	60 00				
104	2/5	State Bank	75 00				183 00
105	2/5	Bill S.	80 00				
106	2/5	United Fund	10 00				93 00
107	2/5	Readers Digest	17 40				75 60
	2/15	Deposit (Bill)				828 00	903 60
108	2/15	Mary S.	440 00				463 00
109	2/15	Sears	40 00				
110	2/15	Electric Co.	41 50				382 10

REMEMBER TO RECORD AUTOMATIC PAYMENTS / DEPOSITS ON DATE AUTHORIZED.

RECORD ALL CHARGES OR CREDITS THAT AFFECT YOUR ACCOUNT

NUMBER	DATE	DESCRIPTION OF TRANSACTION	PAYMENT/DEBIT (-)	√ T	FEE (IF ANY) (-)	DEPOSIT/CREDIT (+)	BALANCE
							382 10
111	2/22	Telephone Co.	28 00				
112	2/22	Visa	87 50				266 60
113	2/22	Citgo Oil	76 00				
114	2/22	Second Finance	37 50				153 10
115	3/24	The Nite Club	38 75				
116	3/25	Rexall	38 75				75 60
117	3/28	United Church	6 00				
118	3/28	Sport Shop	15 00				54 60
119	3/28	Cash (Surplus)	29 60				25 00
		MARCH					
	3/1	Deposit (Bill)				828 00	853 00
120	3/1	Rent	405 00				
121	3/1	Cycle Shop	33 50				414 50

REMEMBER TO RECORD AUTOMATIC PAYMENTS / DEPOSITS ON DATE AUTHORIZED.

60 Minutes of keeping up.

FINANCIAL PLAN WORKSHEET

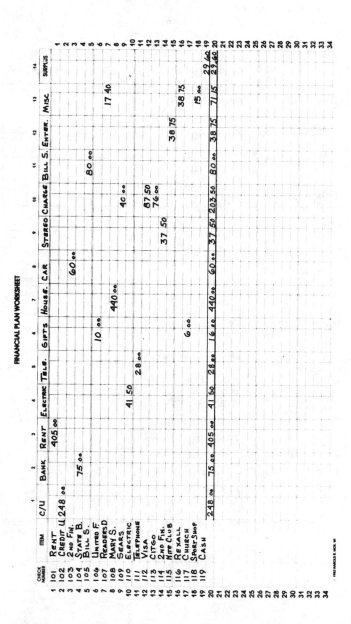

CHECK NUMBER	ITEM	1 C/U	2 BANK	3 RENT	4 ELECTRIC	5 TELE.	6 GIFTS	7 HOUSE.	8 CAR	9 STEREO	10 CHARGE	11 BILL S.	12 ENTER.	13 MISC.	14 SURPLUS
101	RENT			405.00											
102	CREDIT U.	248.00													
103	2ND FIN.														
104	STATE B.		75.00												
105	BILL S.								60.00						
106	UNITED F.											80.00			
107	READERS D						10.00							17.40	
108	MARY S.														
109	SEARS							440.00							
110	ELECTRIC				41.50						40.00				
111	TELEPHONE					28.00									
112	VISA										87.50				
113	CITGO										76.00				
114	2ND FIN.									37.50					
115	NPF CLUB												38.75	38.75	
116	REXALL						6.00								
117	CHURCH														
118	SPORT SHOP													15.00	
119	CASH														
20		248.00	75.00	405.00	41.50	28.00	16.00	440.00	60.00	37.50	203.50	80.00	38.75	71.15	29.60
															29.60

Make Your Paycheck Last

FINANCIAL PLAN

SAVINGS   REAL & PROJECTED

YEAR	JAN	FEB	MAR	APR	MAY	JUN	JUL	AUG	SEPT	OCT	NOV	DEC
CREDIT UNION		248 - / 248 -	248 -	248 -	248 -	248 -						
STATE BANK		75 - / 75 -	75 -	76 -	75 -	75 -						
TOTAL SAVINGS		323 - / 323 -	323 -	323 -	323 -	323 -						

OBLIGATIONS

	JAN	FEB	MAR	APR	MAY	JUN	JUL	AUG	SEPT	OCT	NOV	DEC
RENT		405 - / 405 -	405 -	405 -	405 -	405 -						
ELECTRIC COMPANY		45 - / 41.50	45 -	45 -	45 -	45 -						
TELEPHONE		33 - / 28 -	33 -	33 -	33 -	33 -						
GIFTS AND CONTRIBUTIONS		16 - / 16 -	16 -	16 -	16 -	16 -						
HOUSEHOLD		440 - / 440 -	440 -	440 -	440 -	440 -						
CAR PAYMENT		60 - / 60 -	60 -	60 -	60 -	60 -			52 -			
STEREO PAYMENT		37.50 / 37.50	37.50	37.50	37.50	37.50			26 -			
CHARGE PAYMENT VISA SEARS CITGO		203.50 / 203.50	203.50	203.50	203.50	203.50						
SCHOOL EXPENSE - BILL		80 - / 80 -	80 -	80 -	80 -	80 -						
RECREATION AND ENTERTAINMENT		50 - / 38.75	50 -	50 -	50 -	50 -						
MISC		65 - / 71.15	65 -	65 -	65 -	65 -						

60 Minutes of keeping up.

		1758-	1758-	1758-	1758-	1758-						
TOTAL OBLIGATIONS		1758- 1744⁹⁰										

NET INCOME

BILL		1656- 1656-	1656-	1656-	1656-	1656-			1677-				
MARY		118 - 118-	118 -	118-	118-	118-				148 -	148 -	148 -	
TOTAL INCOME		1774- 1774-	1774-	1774-	1774-	1774-							

SURPLUS

		16 - 29⁶⁰	16 -	16 -	16 -	16 -						

† 1988 HAROLD R. MOE, WI

total obligations. As you can see, the Stevensons' total came to $1,744.40.

Next, Bill and Mary entered their income, which totaled $1,774.

The final breathtaking step is to subtract the "Total Obligations" from the "Total Income" to determine the amount of "Surplus." The Stevensons had a surplus of $29.60, which makes February a smashing success!

It is always interesting to note that, even with a surplus, some obligations will be greater than projected. Your first concern is to maintain a surplus, *any* surplus. Secondly, keep each obligation as near to your original projection as possible. When completing each month, take a moment to compare your projections with the actual dollars spent in each category.

As we discussed earlier, Bill and Mary maintain a $25 buffer in their checking account. At the end of February, they wrote check number 119 to cash (surplus) for $29.60, which left that $25 balance (buffer) at the end of the month (as their check register shows).

How much time was required for the Stevensons to complete their financial plan at the end of the month, recording everything that they spent, figuring their surplus, then writing a check to themselves for that surplus? Certainly less than one hour on February 28th! Spending the $29.60

surplus will probably take them more time!

Save your monthly worksheets. Not only are they a must at tax time, but you'll find them very beneficial for future planning.

Now you have the plan! It's a good one and Chapter 4 will give you some great ideas on fine tuning. See you there!

Remember: Good money management is a little extra work each month, but not *nearly* as much as the work necessary to replace needlessly spent dollars.

CHAPTER 4

WHEN SURPLUS IS SHORTAGE

If your plan balances month after month or only occasionally dips "into the red"—those months when there is "more month than money" left—the strategies discussed in this chapter will help you fine-tune an already workable program. If, however, your financial plan sinks deeper into deficit each month, read this chapter carefully.

Look for the warning signs

Let's begin by looking at the five financial danger signs. These signs will tell you when tough sledding lies ahead. Simply answer "yes" to any of the below questions and consider yourself on the road to trouble. Answer "no" to these questions and you're probably in good shape. (Using the information compiled in constructing your financial plan will be most helpful in answering them accurately.)

1. Does your monthly installment debt payment (credit cards and charge accounts) exceed 20 percent of your net income? *(Do not include your home mortgage.)*

2. Do you find it necessary to regularly use money from savings to pay monthly expenses?

3. Have you begun delaying payments that you once paid promptly?

4. Do you charge everyday expenses?

5. If necessary, would it take you more than a
   year to pay off all outstanding debts (again,
   not including your home mortgage)?

These are important warning signs. The decisions on where and what to cut are very personal.
Only you can make them. No one else should. To
make the wisest choices, let's talk about some of
your options.

Are your goals realistic?

In Chapter 1, I mentioned that your goals will
prove to be realistic when they are tested against
your financial plan. Originally, Bill and Mary
agreed that financial security ($2,000 in the bank)
would be one of their short-term goals. When their
income was divided up, there just wasn't enough
money to go around. It would cost $167 per month
for one year to meet this goal. It was their mutual
decision to include this as a medium goal instead.
The monthly cost was now reduced—over 60
months—to a more manageable (and realistic) $30.
Bill and Mary did not eliminate their goal. They
simply made it realistic for their particular situation.

Review *your* spending goals. Is there enough
money to meet your short-term goal requirements

and your monthly obligations, too? If not, which goals can be put off or delayed to ease your monthly cash flow?

Short-term goals (wants and desires) will generally cause the greatest problems in balancing your new financial plan. That's because short-term wants tend to exceed available income. That means that after monthly obligations are paid, wants seem to consume more than what is left. The only way to deal with this type of situation is to curb your short-term wants. Cut back on monthly spending or spread your short-term wants over a longer time period so they become medium or long-term goals (as the Stevensons did).

As their example showed, changing a short-term goal (one year) to a medium goal (5 years) reduces your monthly cost by 80 percent! However, do not put off until tomorrow what you can do today. Moral: Savings is a must.

Another consideration: Several years into our budget experience, Sandy and I developed a test phrase to help us determine if we really could commit ourselves to a large purchase: "Maintain what you have before you expand." Simple translation: "When there isn't enough money to go around, fix the old first."

Each of us has a little mental list of things we know *should* be done. For example, the car has two bald tires. That's a potentially dangerous situation, and each time you get into your car you think, "We really ought to get a couple of new tires." So what are you doing looking at that new motorcycle? *Maintain* what you have—the needed set of tires for your car—before you *expand* with a new motorcycle.

Each time my neighbor mowed his lawn, he would mentally note that his house needed storm windows. Every winter the cost of heating oil climbed higher and higher, but the acknowledged need for storm windows was only triggered when he looked at his house while mowing (or when he wrote the heating oil check in the cold of winter).

A couple of years ago, Bill's and Mary's beautiful wedding clock sat idle on its living room shelf. Obviously it needed to be cleaned and oiled, which in itself should be a small maintenance task. Since they had an electric kitchen clock, they lived with the inconvenience of not knowing the time while they watched television. Their wedding gift only gathered dust.

Each time Bill brought up the idea of a new component stereo, Mary reminded him that she would prefer to have the clock properly repaired first. With that, the conversation would end.

Neither one got any satisfaction out of their talk. It is interesting to see how easy it would have been for Bill to have gotten Mary's approval for the stereo. But, Bill never remembered to take the clock to the repair shop. Mary was certain it was Bill's responsibility, since he was the person that triggered the "repair-the-clock" thought whenever he talked about a stereo.

From time to time, every person is reminded, if for only a moment, of something that should be attended to. Whether it's tires for the car, storm windows or a clock to be repaired. The importance of these subtle reminders is that they get done in a consistent way. In other words, don't simply ignore them.

To put it in another perspective, consider the new tires. If they are ignored and the motorcycle is purchased, the tires will *not* get any better. Plans have been made so the motorcycle payments can be made without any apparent sacrifice. Then, to our consternation, the car is rendered unusable by tires that are flat and beyond repair. Wouldn't it be wiser to put off the motorcycle for three months or so until the tires are replaced and paid for?

In the case of my neighbor, he was upset by the high heating bills that he knew could be reduced by installing storm windows. He was equally upset by the fact that he had had the money for the windows, but spent it on a snowmobile that a broken track had rendered inoperative. This becomes doubly unfortunate because the money to repair the snowmobile must be used for the additional fuel oil costs.

Maintain what you have (my neighbor's windows), before you expand (the snowmobile should be repaired and enjoyed).

If you *really* have been paying attention, you already realized the Stevensons had their wedding clock repaired—they have a stereo payment entered on the financial plan you looked at in Chapter 2.

Lists aren't just for Santa

I advocate list making. First, because lists organize priorities. When you make a list, you can visually commit yourself to acknowledge what is important. Keeping ideas in your head just doesn't cut it. It's easy to forget or recall ideas in an inappropriate order.

Second, by writing down an idea, you are free to concentrate on other important things—problem-solving, an important project or simply relaxing.

Did you know a grocery list will save 10 percent on food bills by reducing impulse buying?

So far you have made three goal lists, from which you have constructed two savings lists. Using these will enable you to organize and direct your financial efforts in a predetermined direction. A direction you have planned.

But, what about those other "little" things? All those loose ends?

To accommodate a solution, I introduce you to the "To Do" List. A To Do List is for the things you want to make time to get around to. Not goals, but projects you want or need to complete. It's a grab bag of activities, a catchall, if you will. A potpourri of loose ends.

A To Do List is different for each person and each situation. The one similarity, however, is that a To Do List will free up creative energy and allow the user more free time. It makes any financial plan (and home) function with less effort and stress.

A To Do List is not completed by sitting down over a cup of coffee and jotting down everything in 20 minutes. That's a short-term goals list.

A To Do List is done over a longer time period. If you're getting into your car and the bald tires pop into your mind for the tenth time, go straight to your To Do List and write it down.

When you're mowing your lawn and realize storm windows would save heat and money, let the mower run, but write it down on your To Do List. My neighbor should have stopped his mower, walked straight to his desk and put storm windows on his To Do List. Then, finished mowing.

The Stevensons agreed to do the clock repair before the stereo purchase.

How are *your* tires?

Refer to your To Do List when you review your financial plan. Most people with a To Do List will use their surplus when money is needed to complete the project.

As you build your To Do List, do one item each day (or week). No more, no less. On the first of each week, take Item 1 (not 2 or 4) and do what's necessary to complete it by week's end. If any project requires more than a few dollars to complete, consider placing it on one of your goal lists. If it's storm windows, it may be necessary to nail plastic over the windows this year and put the storms on next summer.

The whole idea is (yes, you're ahead of me now!): Maintain what you have before you expand.

What does this have to do with balancing your financial plan? Maintaining what you have will, in most cases, cost less than expanding. Give it some thought. Also, when you expand, you now have two things to maintain. What you had and what you have acquired by expanding.

Making that shortage a surplus

Below are more ideas that will help keep your financial plan working and out of the red:

1. **As a couple, agree on your goals.** This is normally done when goal lists are completed. If there is any disagreement, try to compromise.

2. **Don't start cutting away at one category just because it looks too big.** A major expense cannot be cut simply because it appears "too big" when the amount is computed. Food or Household is a category that most families will try to slash first. If that item is cut too low, the result could become an impossibility, and the money manager won't be able to manage. If the family refuses to eat beans in place of steaks, the cook can't be expected to feed the family on a beans budget.

3. **Try to have a flexible plan and include everyone involved in its success.** Each year, a family's life brings its own special highs and disasters. If your plan is unyielding, it will break from its own inflexibility.

4. **Try to provide everyone involved with an amount they can spend as they see fit.** It may have to be small, but if the entire family

cooperates, the amounts can become larger (it's one way to divide a surplus!). Also, this helps prevent nagging and bickering over money. There won't be any need to dip into the grocery money for lunch with friends or to conceal the real amount of the paycheck in order to have a little money for an evening out with the guys. Instead, everything will be open and aboveboard.

5. **When reductions in spending are unavoidable, consider each category of expense.** Can you reduce Rent? Well, can you get by with less space? If you are single, can you share with someone to cut costs? Heat: Consider insulation, storm windows or cleaning the furnace. Repair Service: Can you do more repairs yourself? Talk to friends and find out how they have reduced costs. Visit your library and public utilities. They have many money-saving ideas for reducing costs.

6. **Don't make a big deal over little things.** Instead, look for trends and discuss these with everyone involved.

7. **Be willing to reevaluate priorities.** You may see a lot of money going for entertainment and clothing, while the family complains that a new couch is needed or the TV is shot. A family

conference may be in order to establish what is
essential and what is a luxury. Keep everyone
involved and remain flexible.

8. If you simply can't stretch the paycheck to
   cover all your monthly obligations for (hopefully) a *short* period of time, **visit your credi-
   tors.** Explain to them what you are doing to
   work out your debts. Seek to adjust your payment schedule if necessary. Show them your
   financial plan. Protect your credit!

9. If you have several installment loans, **consider
   a consolidation loan,** but only from a credit
   union, savings and loan or bank (not a high-
   cost loan company). This will consolidate your
   outstanding debts and enable you to make
   only one monthly payment at a greatly
   reduced amount. Note: Studies have shown
   that four out of five people—**80 percent**—
   who take out such a loan replace their monthly debt load *within 24 months.* It should be
   obvious given this statistic that for a consolidation loan to be effective, taking on additional
   installment payments must be a definite "no-
   no" until the consolidation loan is significantly
   reduced. Remember: You simply *cannot* borrow your way to solvency. A consolidation
   loan is an excellent tool, but like most things,
   it must be used with a sound plan in mind.

10. **The best financial plan may run aground because of family emotional situations.** A spouse may be extremely thrifty—to the point of penny pinching. Someone's psychological difficulties may result in gambling, over-generosity or heedless spending, even after agreement to a plan designed to pay off debts. The person involved may be unable to understand the problem and/or need professional help to eliminate the cause. If you (or a family member) find yourself in this situation, seek help from a family social service agency in the telephone book.

These extraordinary circumstances aside, be confident that most people, once they recognize the possibilities of a sound financial plan, *can and do* eliminate their money problems.

11. **Set up a special place where your records, bills and worksheets are to be kept.** A desk is best (but not required) for organizing bill-paying and maintaining your up-to-date financial plan. Nearly any place will do—just as long as you recognize the importance of setting one up.

A cardboard box just isn't the way to organize bills and worksheets. If space in the family room is a problem, consider a corner of the living room, bedroom, kitchen or hall. What about a desk in the basement? Financial planning is important, and it requires that each family make room for it.

12. Remember: **It's more worthwhile to save a dollar than to add a dollar to your present income.** To add a dollar requires your gross income to increase a minimum of $1.15 (before taxes). When spending is reduced one dollar, you recover a *full* dollar. Even when you bring in more income, you're caught by higher taxes. Your best recourse is better management of the cash you have.

13. **Most people who find themselves in financial hot water are simply overextended.** That means they have used money that should have gone into savings, or have taken money out of savings, or, worse yet, borrowed to cover everyday expenses. If you find yourself overextended, **reduce spending.** Stop using credit, and try not to take on new installment payments. There is life without credit cards! Cool off your spending until you have a surplus to spend.

14. **After using your financial plan for several months, you will know the value of looking for trends.** Look at each expense and determine if it's on target or if you might need

to adjust your projection. If it's a troublemaker, it will do so with a trend first.

15. In troubleshooting your new plan, **it isn't important to maintain absolutely precise records right at the start.** Unless you have always kept exact records, you will have had to estimate to determine your projections. Relax. Later it will be possible to be more precise.

16. **Should you begin to feel the heat of overextension, reexamine your priorities.** You may not be able to save for a vacation and a microwave at the same time.

17. **To keep savings on schedule**, consider using devices such as automatic payroll deductions or monthly transfers from checking to savings.

Do you see yourself side-tracked by any of these 17 financial roadblocks? Any one of them will undermine an otherwise effective financial plan and certainly prevent yours from being all that it can be. Every day, people lose more and more of what they've worked for...just by not seeing the erosion caused by seemingly unimportant attitudes and habits. Never underestimate the obvious—having a special place for your financial records is as important as a consistent savings program. Expecting financial success without first setting worthwhile goals is unworkable. You cannot achieve anything without first setting out the goals you want to achieve.

Many people have a mistaken idea—that life is played much like any game. In baseball, players practice to improve their skills in preparation for next week's game. A good player practices his throwing, his catching, his running and his battling. If this week's game proves not to be a victory, well, it was a good try and next week's contest will surely be better. Practice makes perfect, or so the cliche goes!

The financial game is *different—because there is no practice session*. It's now and it's for *keeps!*

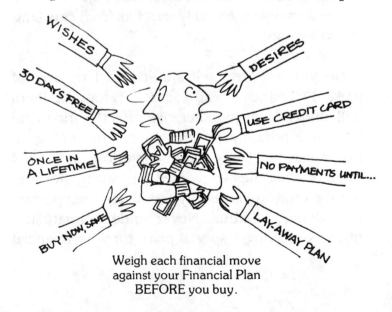

Weigh each financial move
against your Financial Plan
BEFORE you buy.

There is no next time or next week to try again. A bad investment, an unforeseen emergency or an untimely purchase can put you years behind your ability to ever catch up. Sometimes you will never be able to recover. It is important to plan ahead (by setting worthwhile goals), and it is important to weigh each financial decision against your financial plan *before you act*. In a financial sense, you don't get any any practice tries...unless you're willing to pay for them.

This chapter deals with the mystery of not having enough money to go around. It's rather like standing there on pay day, trying to stuff your hard-earned money into your pockets while all these people are trying to keep you from doing it! They want to get as much of your cash as they can. *That's* what our economy is all about... and that can be a problem, one I call "the problem of realization."

The importance of that plan

If you are reading this book, you probably find yourself in one of two distinct situations. The first is something like this: "I make good money, I pay my bills on time, but sometimes I wonder if I can do better. Am I doing all I am capable of?" This is an excellent reason to begin financial planning. It will enable you to fine-tune your spending or, even better, take stock of your total financial situation.

The second conversation goes something like this: "I'm talking hot water here! Real discomfort between me and pay day! I can't even begin to see the tunnel, let alone the light at its end!"

The difference between these two situations is obvious. Someone in the first position already *has* control; he or she wants to *maximize the return*.

The second situation is a real dilemma. This person will need to reevaluate his or her entire program to develop the discipline necessary to follow a sound financial plan.

Whatever your situation, the realization remains the same, whether it's necessary to slap the hands trying to "pick your pockets" on pay day or "just say no" to the enticing ads placed in front of you hundreds of times every day. The answer isn't a budget that tells how you have *already* spent your money, but rather a financial plan that enables you to determine how you *plan* to spend your money.

If you buy this idea, you'll be able to get your pocketful of money home to better decide who gets what part of your money pie.

But as we've previously discussed, before you're able to say *how* you plan to spend (or not spend) your money, you must know *what is important to you.* Sounds simple! There is an old saying that goes, "If you don't know where it is you want to go, you'll likely end up someplace else." Most people just don't know. To make it in this economy, it's absolutely essential to set personal spending goals. This continues to be the single most important step toward financial success anyone can take...yet so few people ever take the time to figure it out.

In our society, we take note of the disadvantaged and applaud any group or agency that lends a helping hand. For each of us, having an income means being able to take care of our needs/proper food, secure shelter and adequate clothing. As you review your goals in the context of this chapter, watch for the truth in this phrase: "Wants expand to consume the available resources!" It will be worthwhile to ask yourself this simple question: "Which of my goals are *wants* and which are *needs*?"

Needs are the unavoidable costs of just being on this planet—from housing, food and clothing to taxes, medical care, transportation, utilities and not a few others. Fortunately the needs list is relatively short, but nonetheless costly. I don't know anyone doing handsprings over paying these unavoidable and necessary obligations.

Wants, on the other hand, are endless! A quick look at your goal lists proves that! The trick is being able to *differentiate* wants from needs so as not to jeopardize your financial future. Life may seem like a game, but you better not play that game with your money. As you review your monthly (and not-so-monthly) obligations, **delay spending for the wants until your needs are taken care of.**

Ferreting out costly wants would seem as easy as attaining your first goal. Well, not really. Anyone who hasn't found a surplus at the end of their financial plan by now has only one place left to look. Actually I have discussed several options beyond the 17 numbered in this chapter. Of all

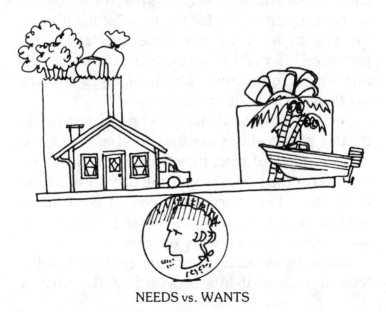

NEEDS vs. WANTS

possible solutions to the dilemma of finding that elusive surplus, there would seem to remain only *two* choices: find more money or reduce your wants.

In reality, that means there is only *one* choice: Since wants expand to consume available resources, more money will prove to be only a temporary solution...at best. Wants vs. needs is all that remains. Why is that such a big deal? Well, needs provide for our existence, while wants provide our lifestyle. That is the bottom line.

It's much like the man who is told by his doctor that either he stops smoking or he won't need next year's calender. Now consider the person who begins an aggressive health program only after he or she suffered a heart attack. It wasn't until his or her lifestyle was threatened that real action took place.

It's not until we come face to face with a possible threat to our *financial* or social lifestyles that serious consideration is given to our financial wants...and any change in our financial lifestyle will undeniably have a corresponding effect on our *social* lifestyle. To put ourselves back on safe financial footing, it will be necessary to clearly identify wants and pressing needs.

If the lack of a surplus has brought you to this point, you now have the only answer left. The best of luck in making these difficult choices!

The way to financial peace of mind goes beyond examples and illustrations. It's not in how much you earn, but what you do with what you earn. Wanting more and more income won't get what you want, but *managing* what you have will. It's not living by some mystical dream, but rather planning how you are going to live.

Your financial plan will tell you your personal financial story. Whether you like the story or not, you still have to listen to it. Whether this version of your financial condition is what you want, it is the *true* version. Be determined and honest, and you will learn the art of making your paycheck last.

Remember: To *do* it you gotta get around *to* it.

CHAPTER 5

I CAN SEE CLEARLY NOW, BUT...

As you continue using your financial plan and become familiar with its operation, questions will arise. Questions about evaluating your new information, maintaining your plan and how to make it work harder for you. In this chapter, we'll discuss the most frequently asked questions.

In dealing with your special questions, the first action should be to reread the section that deals with your problem area. Next, consider your situation. As long as your resulting solution is reasonable, try it. There just aren't any hard and fast rules.

1. Question: When evaluating the success of my plan, how will I know if I'm doing the right things?

Answer: There is no firm yardstick to measure your progress, but there *are* two basic indicators to use. Both are related to trends that develop month by month. The first, your surplus, is the most important. If you consistently have a surplus, your plan is doing what it is expected to do. Even when your surplus is small, your plan can still be considered successful. Chapter 4 is devoted to ways of *ensuring* a surplus. Review this chapter if you don't have a positive surplus any two consecutive months.

Also, by not writing that check for your monthly surplus, you can cause your plan to go into the red the following month. The importance of this was discussed at the end of Chapter 2. Review this section from time to time.

What about the months where there is a surplus but several obligations exceed their original projections? That's when our second indicator, fine-tuning, is necessary. If actual costs continually exceed projections by more than 15 percent, a conference with everyone involved is in order. Talk it over, openly discuss ways of cutting back to return to your projections. If the original projections are based on estimates, it may be necessary to reevaluate these figures.

By discussing these projections, everyone involved is alerted to the overages. An honest and tactful discussion will provide ideas and a new resolve to keep each projection on target.

Fine-tuning, zeroing in on each obligation is important. But, the bottom line—your monthly surplus—should be your first concern. If the surplus is, by your estimate, unusually large, it might be a good idea to increase savings. Too large a surplus leads to complacency, which in itself makes your financial plan less than it could be. A reasonable surplus is necessary— the exact amount you consider acceptable is up to you.

If your To Do List is long, you may want to plan for a slightly larger surplus.

Generally, a surplus of 3 to 5 percent of your net income is a good average (3 percent of a net income of $1,000 is $30). If your surplus is more than 5 percent, think about reducing it. A little extra in savings will go a long way on rainy days. When it's continually less than 3 percent, zero in on fine-tuning each obligation.

2. **Question: When evaluating the success of my plan, what is the most important aspect to consider?**

Answer: Goals! Without goals, as I've stressed again and again, no plan will be effective. No matter how elaborate it might be, no matter how well-intentioned, it will not be effective or lasting without first having a goal. Goals provide direction, priorities and momentum. Without these, there is no lasting reason to stay with a program. Without first having the goal, there can be no planned success. Your financial plan is, in one sense, simply the *means by which you achieve the goals you set for yourself.*

In evaluating your progress on a monthly basis, you can see where your surplus and fine-tuning are important. What about the long run? Next year and the following? The top priority of every financial plan must be a consistent savings goal. It may only be $5 per month, but *consistently* saving an amount, no matter how small, is what it's all about. I don't think it's necessary to go into a discussion of the needs and virtues of saving for tomorrow, but it is well to consider the poor hands that life can occasionally deal each of us. Realize that a savings program can spell the difference between surviving a momentary crisis or temporarily falling backward.

So when evaluating your plan, be confident your goals are worthy. They reflect how you want to direct your time and resources. Then, be certain your priorities include absolute consistency in your two savings programs. As you review your spending month after month, your plan will enable you to answer three questions: "Where do you *want* your money to go?" "Where *should* your money go?" "Where *does* your money go?"

3. **Question: I just started my financial plan and already have $100 in my short-term savings. Yesterday my auto insurance bill arrived for $300. What do I do now that I am $200 short?**

   Answer: What did you do *before* you had a savings account (which now has $100 in it)? Did you cut back on a number of monthly obligations to free up the needed cash? Since you are just getting your plan started, you may want to do just that.

Some people use a different approach. If they are saving $150 a month in their short-term savings account, they will save $1,800 each year. In order to get their fledgling plan off the ground, one option is to borrow that $1,800 from the bank and repay it at $150 per month. The interest paid on this loan will be partially offset by the interest earned on the savings. (A better way might be to borrow only $500 or $600 on a one-year note to give you seed money for your account, instead of borrowing the full $1,800.)

Another possible solution is a "Peter-to-Paul" loan. Borrow the $200 you're short from your long-term savings account. You are robbing Peter to pay Paul, with "Peter" being your opportunity account. I favor one of the other methods since this arrangement can be habit-forming. However, a Peter-to-Paul loan is an option.

These are three possible solutions. Consider your situation, then look at your options.

4. **Question: Our financial plan had a surplus 8 months out of 12. What suggestions do**

you have regarding the four months there was no surplus?

Answer: Upon reviewing your plan, I noticed that if you had paid nothing more than the amount projected for charge payments and medical, you would have had a perfect 12 months. If you are free of medical bills for several months and get a $50 office call, pay only the $20 you projected. Next month, pay $20. The month after that, pay the final $10.

Charge accounts do require more attention because of minimum payment requirements. Still, that's a good reason to limit time payments. Because of the advantages that go with charge accounts, it's a good idea to treat them with a special watchfulness.

While reviewing the financial plan used in this question, it will be helpful to mention one other observation. The short-term savings account includes a monthly amount toward insurance. Since a particular insurance payment was only $75, it was paid from the primary checking account and shown as a Miscellaneous obligation on the financial plan. That's fine, because the insurance payment was made and all is well. However, that meant that Miscellaneous jumped from $45 to $120, while your savings dropped terribly ($75) for the month. When making future projections, entries like this can get a little confusing...if not downright scary.

Therefore, when making payments that normally should come from savings, enter the payment in savings on your worksheet—*not* in Miscellaneous, *even if you pay it by check from your primary account.*

5. **Question: Each month I total my financial plan and determine my surplus. Then, I write a check for that sum. Since I have the amount of surplus recorded on my plan and check register, why do I have a "Surplus" column on my worksheet?**

Answer: First, your surplus should equal your checkbook balance (plus any buffer). Once your check for surplus has been written, your checking balance will be zero (or the amount of your buffer if you use one). If there is a difference between your checkbook balance and the surplus amount, use your checkbook balance since it is reduced to zero each month (assuming your math is correct).

Why do you have a "Surplus" column on your worksheet? Because your worksheet is actually a large check register, with a couple of modifications. Instead of simply subtracting checks and adding deposits (as you do with a check register), your worksheet also categorizes checks. However, like your check register, continuity is maintained by check number.

Another advantage offered by the worksheet is at tax time. Necessary checks are easy to find if you search by category *first* (e.g., Medical or Mortgage), *then* locate checks by number.

More about this later.

6. **Question: You have talked a lot about list-making and its value in selecting the best option when making a financial decision. Would you briefly outline this process?**

   Answer: Volumes have been written on the decision-making process. When all is said and done, it can be reduced to a five-step method. Whether we are aware of it or not, each decision we make is in some way achieved through this five-step process.

   To illustrate, imagine you have a large heating oil bill that must be paid within 30 days. Here's how the decision-making process works.

   1. **Define your problem.**
      The best problem-solving is done on paper. By writing things down, you're able to view the problem in a form other than passing

thoughts. I have a huge $600 oil bill to pay in 30 days with only $200 available!

2. **Consider your capabilities and strong points**

   How much cash do I have and where is it? Examine checking and savings accounts. What bills can be put off or minimums paid? Is there any additional money coming in the next 30 days? Assess your strong points: Overtime, part-time work, etc. Now may be the time to sell your neighbor the antique clock he has been panting for. Lastly, consider asking the oil company about time payments—you know you can budget $110 per month for fuel oil.

3. **Identify the problems in reaching your goal**

   You have the flu.

4. **Consider your options**
   a. Take $200 out of savings and/or...
   b. Use the $50 cash on hand and/or...
   c. Minimum payments on current bills (an additional $75) and/or
   d. The oil company will accept payment over 90 days.

5. **Select the best option(s)**
   a. Pay over 90 days. Use the $200 in savings for the first installment payment.

From the information given, how would you make the next two installments?

1. Define the problem

2. Consider your capabilities and strong points

3. Identify problems in reaching your goal

4. Consider your options

5. Select best option

7. **Question: Would you review the ways to determine if your goals are realistic and what can be done if you discover they aren't?**

Answer: Assume your only goal is to pay your monthly bills. First, total your bills to see if there is enough cash to go around. If there is, you have a realistic goal. If not, consider your options: a consolidation loan, monthly installments, etc. (see Chapter 4).

But, let's imagine your goal lists are 10 each and you could add a bunch more, Well, the conclusion is obvious. By making the three goal lists, you can plainly identify what you're after. If it's heavily "money-oriented" and you don't have that kind of cash, realizing it now will enable you to begin planning for it. Maybe you can't achieve everything as soon as you thought, but now you can arrange your priorities and do something positive to bring you closer to those goals...even if closer is now five years away.

One final point: If you really want a vacation home (for example) and find that once you have placed a dollar value on it, it just doesn't seem doable, don't shrug it off as the impossible dream. It might be that actual saving can't begin for eight or nine years. Perhaps the vacation home will result from the equity in your present home. Shelving a goal until the children are out of school can be smart planning.

8. Question: What is the biggest mistake today's wage earners make in managing their money?

Answer: Not planning, or taking a passive approach to money management. Too many people (like their parents before them) assume hard work will automatically pay off with a better job, more income, the house and everything that goes with the Great American Dream. The times have changed, and the rules are different. Young and old alike just aren't geared to using a cash–monitoring plan (a financial plan, if you prefer) to get a clear picture of current income and outflow.

Another error begins to appear as people react to these new rules. Simply put, you just don't spend money for the sake of saving on taxes. It doesn't work and you could go broke doing it. There has got to be a better reason than saving on taxes to spend money. Tax saving should only be a side benefit.

9. **Question: How will this program help me at tax time?**

Answer: Your financial plan will be a great help at tax time. Not only do you have a record by check number of where your money has gone, but it is already divided by category on your worksheet. Talk to your tax preparer to determine which categories will be of benefit to you. Depending on your situation, a portion of your rent, mortgage interest, utilities, medical bills, charitable contributions, charge account interest, auto expense, childcare and more may be tax-deductible.

As your canceled checks are returned from your bank, staple them to the receipts from which they where paid. Then, put these in a manila envelope. Many people label their envelopes, one for each column of their worksheet.

Give your tax preparer the following:

1. W-2 form from your employer

2. The IRS tax guide (arrives in the mail)

3. Your financial plan stapled to the worksheets

4. Envelopes containing your canceled checks and receipts

5. Statement of interest earned in your savings account

6. Don't forget your short-term savings account. Include your copy of your paid property tax bill, insurance bills, organization dues, bank interest, tuition, heating oil bills, etc. Put these in separate envelopes marked "Savings." These are the big obligations you save a little for each month.

That's it! As you can see, you can easily maximize your deductions with good record-keeping. With these good records, you will also minimize the *time* spent collecting the information.

10. Question: What if I don't have a regular income? I work on commission, and my income varies month to month.

Answer: In situations where income varies, you financial plan will really be beneficial. Deposit your commission in a savings account or interest-bearing checking account. Each month withdraw the amount you have projected for your "Total Obligations."

This method has a couple of nice advantages. First, you will be receiving interest on the maximum amount of money right up to the time you need it for your monthly obligations. Secondly, with a sound financial plan, it will be easy to know what your dollar needs are for the months down the road.

One note of caution. With an irregular income, it is very important to take great care when estimating your future obligations so that during the low-income months the cash is there.

11. Question: What do you think of the use of credit cards?

Answer: Credit is a valuable asset that becomes a liability with overuse.

Credit is important to have in this day and age. It offers a reserve that you can fall back on when an emergency arises. It offers the flexibility that enables you to take advantage of sales and avoid future price increases. Durable goods like refrigerators, washing machines and cars can be financed as necessary. Vacations, gifts, everyday expenses and purchases under $25 shouldn't be paid with credit (assuming they are not for business purposes).

You should always remember that most financial crises start with the unwise use of credit.

Here are some safety rules for taking full advantage of credit while keeping out of hot water:

1. **Don't seek more credit than you need.** A critical analysis of your financial plan will give you a pretty good feel for your credit requirements.

   Even though you think you will use it only in an emergency, the temptation is always there. Also, unused credit is sometimes counted against you when you seek large credit—i.e., a home or auto loan—since use of this unused credit could possibly affect your ability to repay the loan you now seek.

2. **Don't expand your use of credit simply because your income increases.** It is far better to use extra income to reduce your present debt load.

3. **Keep the number of non-business credit cards to a minimum.** Credit counselors advise their clients to carry no more than two cards. The more you have, the more the psychological tendency to overspend. The other advantage is not so obvious. Credit cards in most states charge interest of about 18 percent on the first $500, then 12

percent on amounts over $500. The fewer cards you use, the less interest you will pay on the same amount of dollars charged.

4. **Never charge any item under $25.** A significant amount of bad debt stems from small purchases...that probably would never have been made if the person had paid cash.

5. **Never charge everyday expenses.** Never!

6. **Use your financial plan to determine the amount you can comfortably afford** to devote to credit card repayment. Then monitor your credit purchases carefully so your comfort level is never exceeded.

7. Excluding mortgage payments, **loan repayment (credit card and charge accounts) should not exceed 20 percent** of an individual's or couple's take-home pay.

Use credit wisely and it will offer you a great deal of flexibility. You will realize that your income will indeed go further and yield a greater return.

12. **Question: As a new money manager, my financial situation is clearly improving. That's great. How else can I make my paycheck go further?**

Answer: The ways to stretch your paycheck are abundant and limited only by your inclination. Here are a few ideas to help you get started.

The cash discount is a real money saver used by all successful people. It works two ways. First, when buying *anything,* ask for a 10-percent discount. Sound ridiculous?

Hold on! I know people who expect 20 percent. I am only suggesting 10 until you gain confidence!

The other angle of the cash discount goes like this: Suppose you plan to paint your house. You missed the traditional paint sale in September. Go to the paint store, pick out the color you want and explain what you are about to do (the painting, not the money savings). Now, look the owner or manager (never a clerk) in the eye and say, "If you will sell me paint at the contractors' discount, I'll give you all of my business from now on!" You have just saved anywhere from 20 percent to 40 percent. *That* certainly makes your paycheck go further.

When buying large items, such as appliances and furniture, shop around and always ask, "And what is my discount?" Be serious, and you won't go to three stores before you have what you're after at a big savings. I say three stores because two will certainly give you 10 percent. It's the third store that will save you 15 percent to 20 percent (or more). This money-saving idea is used by dollar-wise people, and it will work for you.

Locally owned, neighborhood stores are most receptive to discounting. Particularly if they are assured you will be a dependable, repeat customer.

I know a fellow who saves 10 percent at his local hardware store using this approach. Not only does he save 10 percent, but since he is a frequent, repeat buyer, the store bills him each month. That's convenient. He has assured me his average discount is much higher since he is offered super deals on damaged, discontinued and returned merchandise.

However, don't think for a moment that major stores won't give discounts. They can't be as flexible and won't include all store items, but because of their buying power, their sales offer tremendous savings. In larger cities, chain stores have outlets where slightly damaged, discontinued and overstock merchandise is sold at up to 50 percent off.

When we talked about list-making, I said that a grocery list will save 10 percent by eliminating impulse buying. Additionally, shopping once or twice a month will reduce exposure to impulse buying. Unless you have a particular purchase in mind, try to stay out of stores. Window shopping can be expensive.

Another money-saving, paycheck-stretching idea is "doing it yourself." Not everything, but a few things. Hardware stores and lumberyards give free advice. Utility companies and magazines are full of ideas and directions. Neighbors are surprisingly ingenious. Talk to them and you'll have fun at the same time.

A discount of 10 percent here, 20 percent there. Hey, it all adds up. Try it!

As you can see, financial planning is no mystery and certainly not just for the old and rich. The entire economy has undergone fantastic changes in the past few years. Clearly, it will never be the same as it was. Having your financial plan will provide the means to weather the economic downturns and take advantage of the better times that are sure to follow.

One of the changes that has taken place in our economy is the way banking is done. In my view, the deregulation of the banking industry has been for the better. Today, financial institutions pay interest on checking account balances, while just a few years ago, there wasn't the competition between lenders for any of them to consider products like a "free" account. Today there is.

Of all the changes to come over the horizon, the rapid growth of credit unions has to be the most significant, and for good reason. Just about every community, profession, trade and organization can claim a credit union. Imagine that! All these people with a common interest, pooling their financial resources for the benefit of each member. Benefits from higher interest on their savings to lower interest for loans, to special considerations because of the unique components of the membership group. It's like the birds of a feather flocking together idea in action. Without a doubt, credit unions are doing more to change the way banking is done today than any other force in our economy. I believe the reason for their tremendous success is not only the "we care about you" attitude, but their strong, competitive, service-oriented ideas. I recommend that if you haven't already taken the time, check credit unions out.

It's a fact. In today's seesaw economy, an effective cash-monitoring system is critical. If you've been slow in getting started with your financial plan, I encourage you to take the time to identity your goals and write them down. If you've read this far without even starting your plan because you've decided to pay off your Visa card or some other bill first, think about this: You can't pay off your obligations without first having a plan you're committed to. You didn't use a plan to get into the situation you now are working to get free from. If you choose to begin paying your obligations without first committing yourself to a plan, it is quite likely you will never succeed. You haven't given yourself good enough reasons to change your practices.

Paying your bills off before developing a sound plan is like old Scrooge saving money for savings' sake. He became a victim of his savings. That same thing can happen to anyone who intends to pay their debts off first.

Complete the steps outlined in this book. Keep going, one step at a time. Once completed, concentrate only on the first month. When you make it through the first month, let the person (you) with a full month of experience decide how the following month will be handled. Let it happen.

Studies prove that establishing a new habit requires repetition over a period of time. This is true of any new discipline, be it an exercise program, dieting or developing a new skill. In a financial sense, this means eliminating potential self-defeating spending habits and establishing goal-oriented practices. Anything worthwhile takes time to develop; it can't happen overnight.

When we first started, if I had believed that I only needed to pay off my debts, I wouldn't have gotten to where I am today. Short-term thinking will pay off today's bills, but getting what you want from life requires long-term thinking.

How did I get started and keep going? Simply put, by working on new habits and maintaining my new discipline one month at a time, for one year at a time. Now, I can't imagine living any other way. Looking back and seeing the things it's provided us, I realize it hasn't all been easy. However, at times the humor was priceless. Living any other way seems so stressful. I wouldn't trade the experience, and what it has done for us as a family, for anything.

Hey, back then I discovered a person could go broke just as easily making $5,000 a month as someone making $1,000 a month. How? Spend $6,000 a month! It's just not that hard to do. No matter how much you earn, it's not what you make that counts, it's what you do with what you make that counts. And the doing is done one month at a time. That's what's so remarkable!

When it becomes necessary to reinforce you or your plan, make a date with your spouse and go to dinner. Discuss your concerns and the progress being made toward your goals. Doing this is a very good strategy, because it gets everyone on neutral ground. Whether we are aware of it or not, we all have our turf to protect. Protected turf is the kitchen where I would never consider asking Sandy about her spending. On the other hand, mine might be my office, where Sandy wouldn't consider giving me a pep talk about my spending or questioning my financial wisdom.

Your favorite restaurant puts people in neutral territory, which enables everyone to relax and be less protective of their actions and opinions. Decisions made in this atmosphere seem to be viewed with greater regard than those made on familiar turf. That's part of what getting along should be about. (The neutral ground technique works. I don't know why. It's one of those mysteries. All I know is, it does.)

Your financial growth (growing pains and all) should always be worth a celebration and not be the source of confrontation. Besides, nobody has to do the dishes after an enjoyable dinner.

You can't make a date for dinner because you're single? No problem. I recommend this exercise to everyone: Remember your favorite vacation. It could have been on a sandy beach or lakeside mountain retreat. Wherever that place is, take a pad and pencil and spend one full day focused on yourself (or selves) and where you want to be in 1, 5 and 15 years. Seldom does anyone actually set aside just one full day to plan their future. Most people spend more time buying a new car then thinking about where they want to be in 10 years.

Why did you get up today? Why did you go to work this week? That's a good question. Where is it going to get you in five years? Where would you *like* to be in five years? What plans do you have for getting there? Ask yourself if you are today where you wanted to be five years ago. Why?

If you're bummed by a job that you've outgrown, why not change? Ask yourself, "What would I do with my time if it were mine?"

Everyone should invest a day of their lives looking at where they've been and where they want their lives to go. Few people ever do. Listen to the answers and they can become your goals, or better yet, your reasons for doing what you do.

For me, my place is a big granite rock just outside Bar Harbor, Maine. It's the ideal place for me to devote 24 hours to planning my next five years. Think about it. Why not take a weekend and invest 24 hours in your future?

Your success will be determined largely by your ability to effectively decide what it is you're willing to give up in order to have what you really want—the big trade-off. By allowing yourself the opportunity to spend 24 hours planning, you'll focus effectively on your future choices. You'll discover options previously unknown to you, which will enable you to avoid less important distractions that drain your resources, distract and sidetrack real progress.

Your goal lists and financial plan are very much like a road map, without which you would certainly make many wrong turns and likely end up at the wrong destination. You now have them to help you get to your destination.

You have the tools you need to set your course, keep control and make your paycheck last!

Remember: There are always possibilities.

INDEX